Partitura
seu
Tabulatura italica

Recent Researches in Music

A-R Editions publishes seven series of critical editions, spanning the history of Western music, American music, and oral traditions.

Recent Researches in the Music of the Middle Ages and Early Renaissance
   Charles M. Atkinson, general editor

Recent Researches in the Music of the Renaissance
   James Haar, general editor

Recent Researches in the Music of the Baroque Era
   Christoph Wolff, general editor

Recent Researches in the Music of the Classical Era
   Eugene K. Wolf, general editor

Recent Researches in the Music of the Nineteenth and Early Twentieth Centuries
   Rufus Hallmark, general editor

Recent Researches in American Music
   John M. Graziano, general editor

Recent Researches in the Oral Traditions of Music
   Philip V. Bohlman, general editor

Each edition in *Recent Researches* is devoted to works by a single composer or to a single genre. The content is chosen for its high quality and historical importance, and each edition includes a substantial introduction and critical report. The music is engraved according to the highest standards of production using the proprietary software MusE, owned by Music│Notes.™

For information on establishing a standing order to any of our series, or for editorial guidelines on submitting proposals, please contact:

A-R Editions, Inc.
801 Deming Way
Madison, Wisconsin 53717

800 736-0070 (U.S. book orders)
608 836-9000 (phone)
608 831-8200 (fax)
http://www.areditions.com

Johann Klemm

Partitura seu Tabulatura italica

Edited by John O. Robison

 A-R Editions, Inc.
Madison

A supplement to this volume, containing keyboard arrangements of the fugues, is available from the publisher.

A-R Editions, Inc., Madison, Wisconsin 53717
© 1998 by A-R Editions, Inc.

A-R Editions is pleased to support scholars and performers in their use of *Recent Researches* material for study or performance. Subscribers to any of the *Recent Researches* series, as well as patrons of subscribing institutions, are invited to apply for information about our "Copyright Sharing Policy."

Printed in the United States of America

ISBN 0-89579-420-9
ISSN 0484-0828

♾ The paper used in this publication meets the minimum requirements of the American National Standard for Information Sciences—Permanence of Paper for Printed Library Materials, ANSI Z39.48-1984.

Contents

Introduction

The Composer

Johann Klemm (c.1595–1659) was born in the Saxon town of Oederan, near Dresden, and served as a choirboy in the Dresden Hofkapelle by 1605, when he was approximately ten years of age. He lived at a time when the Saxon electors Johann Georg I and Johann Georg II, who ruled at the Dresden court from 1611–1656 and 1656–1680, respectively, had one of the most splendid musical establishments in Western Europe. After attaining some status as a court instrumentalist there by 1612, Klemm was sent to Augsburg in 1613 for study with Christian Erbach.[1] Since this study with Erbach was financed by Johann Georg I, Klemm must have shown considerable potential as an organist. He probably also received some instruction in counterpoint and composition from Erbach, and may have learned much from this well-known composer of imitative keyboard works (ricercars, fantasias, and canzonas).[2]

Klemm evidently did not return to Dresden until 1616 or 1617. A letter from Johann Georg I to Landgrave Moritz of Hesse-Kassel, dated 25 April 1615, requests that Schütz be loaned to the Saxon court for two years. The elector's reason for this request was that his musicians had been sent "to Italy and elsewhere" for training. It is unlikely that Schütz's services would have been requested for such a lengthy period if Klemm was expected to complete his studies with Erbach in 1615.[3] Upon his return to Dresden, Klemm began studying composition with Schütz, who in 1617 became a permanent musician in the Dresden musical establishment. As a result of Schütz's two visits to Italy, Klemm would also have been exposed to contemporary Italian music.[4] Klemm was appointed court organist in 1625.[5]

As Kapellmeister, Schütz's energies were geared towards the composition and direction of music for high feast days and festive occasions; as one of Dresden's court organists, Klemm would have, by comparison, been a participant in more ordinary musical occasions, such as weekly church services.[6] During the Thirty Years' War (1618–48), every Dresden musician must have experienced the improvement, decline, and rebuilding of the Dresden Hofkapelle. Between 1632 and 1639, the Hofkapelle membership decreased from thirty-nine to ten members; it then increased to twenty-one musicians by 1647.[7] An organist such as Klemm would probably have been burdened with a good share of everyday musical activities at a time of financial hardship, when musicians were often not paid on time.

There are several indications that Klemm was on excellent terms with Schütz. Klemm's letter (dated 9 March 1646) to his Bautzen colleague, Johann Samuel Schein, indicates that he knew not only when Schütz had visited Leipzig and Weissenfels, but also that Schütz had recommended Schein to "many distinguished persons" in Leipzig.[8] From around the same time, there is also an undated memorandum written by Schütz stating that Klemm should be given part of the responsibility for educating the court's choirboys.[9] Both letters indicate a collegial relationship between the two musicians. Finally, Klemm, along with colleagues in Bautzen and Leipzig, became a music publisher; two of the most important publications resulting from this activity were Schütz's *Sacrae Symphoniae II* (1647) and *Geistliche Chormusik* (1648).[10]

Gina Spagnoli has found evidence that Klemm lived at least eight years longer than scholars had previously assumed. Alexander Silbiger and Friedrich Wilhelm Riedel both state that the last recorded evidence of Klemm at the Dresden court dates from 1651, and that he died in or shortly after 1651.[11] However, Klemm is still listed as a member of the elector's ensemble in 1654–55, as well as a participating musician in the funeral services for Johann Georg I that took place in February of 1657.[12] The most likely date of Klemm's death is 1659, since he is listed as a member of Johann Georg II's musical establishment until this year.[13]

The Context of the *Partitura seu Tabulatura italica*

Overviews of the baroque fugue have focused primarily on the achievements of three individuals working in the first half of the seventeenth century—Frescobaldi, Sweelinck, and Samuel Scheidt.[14] While these composers made outstanding contributions to the development of imitative instrumental music during the early baroque era, a complete picture of the seventeenth-century fugue will only be possible when certain neglected sources are made available to both scholars and performers. This edition of Klemm's *Partitura seu Tabulatura italica* will enhance understanding of the fugue by focusing on the way in which the fugue was perceived at the court of Dresden during the time of Schütz.[15]

Klemm's *Partitura seu Tabulatura italica* was published in Dresden in 1631, the same year that Saxony entered the Thirty Years' War. The collection, which is comprised of thirty-six fugues, includes a two-, three-, and four-part fugue in each of the twelve modes, in the ordering established by Zarlino in the earlier editions of his *Le istitutioni harmoniche*.[16] Like the organ collections of Scheidt and Johann Ulrich Steigleder published during the 1620s, the *Partitura* is printed in open-score format, rather than in the more common German organ tablature.[17] The open-score format is significant for two reasons: first, it indicates that Klemm's collection is partly pedagogical in nature by clearly delineating the individual polyphonic lines in relation to one another, and, second, it allows considerable flexibility in terms of performing medium.

In the postscript, Klemm says that the individual voices have been written out on separate staves so that they can be played on whatever instruments the performers desire.[18] He also indicates on the title page that they are not only for organ, but for all sorts of instruments. While such flexibility was a practical necessity at the time of the Thirty Years' War, Klemm's fugues are effective when played on a variety of string and wind consorts. The individual lines are conjunct with occasional figurations and leaps, and usually do not exceed the range of a twelfth.

When performed on the organ, one wonders what role Klemm's fugues might have played in Dresden church services. While his fugues could have served as preludes or postludes to liturgical services, or as Communion music during the Holy Eucharist, their conservative, heavily imitative style would have been considered appropriate for a variety of occasions.

Although he credits his teacher Schütz with instigating the work, Klemm's fugues are essentially *stile antico* works. One indication of this is his statement in the preface that he has used chromaticism and diminution in a restrained manner.[19] Klemm also indicates that his fugues had been heard as rhetorical exercises presented at public meetings.[20]

By the time Klemm's *Partitura* was published in 1631, the idea of writing a series of contrapuntal instrumental works in the various modes was more than a century old. The first compositions of this nature were Thomas Stoltzer's *Octo Tonorum Melodiae*, a set of eight five-part imitative instrumental pieces, one in each of the modes recognized by early-sixteenth-century theorists.[21] From the early seventeenth century, there is also Costanzo Antegnati's organ print of 1608, which consists of a ricercar in each of the twelve modes. Klemm's teacher Christian Erbach should also be mentioned, since Erbach composed at least two ricercars in each of the first nine modes.[22]

The fugues in Klemm's *Partitura* have equal merit as individual works of art and as pedagogical tools. In this respect, they may be compared with Costanzo Festa's counterpoint studies on a cantus firmus, which could have been useful for learning how to compose, to play in all clefs, to sing, and to play instruments.[23] From two centuries after Festa's studies, Bach's *Well-Tempered Clavier* should also be mentioned, since it is a collection of preludes and fugues systematically covering all major and minor keys. Falling midway between these two examples, Klemm's collection demonstrates how to write a two-, three-, and four-part fugue in each of the twelve modes. And like Festa's studies, Klemm's fugues can be used to develop one's facility both on instruments and in clef-reading. Through the *Partitura* fugues, one can learn a great deal about the composition of good fugue subjects, the melodic and rhythmic alteration of these subjects, the creation of fugal expositions, and the procedures following these expositions.

Formal Characteristics of the Fugues

Subjects

To be perceived as a definite entity, a fugue subject needs to take up a moderate length of time, longer than the head-motives of earlier ricercars and fantasias and not so long that it cannot be easily remembered. Most of Klemm's fugue subjects are two to three bars in length, which is typical of imitative instrumental music dating from the early seventeenth century. The concluding note of the subject is usually placed on the first or third beat of the measure, a procedure that helps to further define the subject. Since the beginning and concluding notes of the subjects are positioned on either the first or third beat of the measure, Klemm's barlines do not imply metrical stress.[24] Twelve of Klemm's fugue subjects are two measures in length plus a downbeat, eight are two and one-half measures long and end on the third beat, and five subjects are three measures in length. The subject of *Fuga XXII* is somewhat unusual, since its last note is placed on the fourth beat of the second measure and sustained through the beginning of the next measure. The remainder have subjects that are more than three and one-half measures in length, the longest of which is over four and one-half measures in length.

Although the melodic curves of the subjects vary, one of their most common characteristics is an emphasis on the fifth scale degree of the mode. Some subjects have static melodic curves centering around the fifth scale degree (for example, *Fuga IX*), while others hover around the fifth scale degree before descending to the final of the mode (for example, *Fuga I* and *Fuga XV*). Two fugue subjects are centered around the fifth scale degree without fitting either of these patterns: the subject in *Fuga XIX* revolves around the fifth scale degree but ends on the sixth scale degree, while the subject of *Fuga XVIII* concludes with a descent from the fifth to the third scale degree. Some subjects also outline the members of the triad built upon the final of the mode (for example, *Fuga VI*), reflecting the early-seventeenth-century theoretical advice that a mode is determined by the first, third, and fifth scale degrees.[25] Many of Klemm's subjects, in their tendency to melodically outline the fifth or fourth of the modal scale, reflect the theoretical advice of Girolamo Diruta, Adriano Banchieri, and Giovanni Maria Trabaci. But there are some that follow the more archaic practice of outlining the fifth or fourth of the mode only by the initial notes of the first two entries of the subject.[26] Thus *Fuga IX* outlines the fifth of the aeolian mode with the inital notes of its first two entries, but the opening two entries of the subject outline only the third to sixth scale degrees and the sixth to second degrees of the mode, respectively. While most fugue subjects have limited ranges, there are four subjects that have unusually large ranges spanning an entire octave (for example, *Fuga XII*).

Fuga IV uses the same subject as the "Recercar terzo" from Frescobaldi's 1626 publication of keyboard works.[27] The opening subject of *Fuga XXVII* uses essentially the same melodic pattern, but is based on the fifth rather than the first scale degree. These two fugues by Klemm in the hypophrygian and phrygian modes are not by any means copies of Frescobaldi's work, but entirely different works that happen to use a commonplace idea. *Fuga XXVIII* has virtually the same subject as a fugue in the phrygian mode by Simon Lohet, whose music Klemm may have known.[28]

In ten fugues, Klemm uses two subjects that are contrasting melodically and rhythmically, answering steps with leaps and long note values with shorter notes. *Fuga XVI*, for example, has an ascending stepwise subject that is followed by a short triadic one; *Fuga XXVII* has a second subject that uses quicker note values than the first subject. Further, two subjects are often presented together initially, and then used independently as a fugue progresses. An excellent example of this tendency is seen in *Fuga XXX*, where the second subject (the stepwise eighth notes first heard in m. 4) is heard in the soprano line in measure 11, long before the first subject is ever presented in that part. *Fuga XXXI* has two rhythmically contrasting subjects that are initially combined to form one subject that is two and one-half measures in length, but after the first two voices have entered, the second of these subjects is used independently on many occasions. An interesting parallel can be made here with Johann Adam Reincken's discussion of fugue dating from 1670, which describes writing a double fugue in which the two subjects may be treated together, separately, and simultaneously against one another.[29]

There does not appear to be a strong relationship between mode and affect in Klemm's fugue subjects, although some tendencies in this direction should be noted. As Joel Lester points out, Lippius and other theorists stated that cheerful or sad affects were determined by the quality of the thirds and sixths over both the final and fifth scale degrees of the mode (minor for sad affects and major for cheerful ones).[30] With the exception of his *Fuga XVI*, all of Klemm's fugues in the phrygian and hypophrygian modes have subjects outlining an upper neighbor tone that lies a semitone above either the first or fifth scale degrees of the mode. Conversely, two fugues in the hypoionian mode (*Fuga XII* and *Fuga XXXVI*) create a somewhat cheerful affect through the use of a series of ascending steps as well as diminutions.

Expositions

In his fugal expositions, Klemm achieves a considerable amount of variety, which is more readily seen in his three- and four-part fugues than in his twelve duos. The two-part fugues generally begin with two entries of the subject centering on the first and fifth scale degrees, followed by several measures of free material leading to a cadence. One exception to this scheme is *Fuga I*, which duplicates the subject a fourth below. Two fugues (*Fuga II* and *Fuga VI*) begin with three or four statements of the subject before reaching a cadence.

Seven of the three-part fugues begin with three entries of the subject that have little free material between them, followed quickly by a cadence (for example, *Fuga XXII* and *Fuga XXIII*). Although some of these expositions have entries on alternate pitches ($\hat{1}$–$\hat{5}$–$\hat{1}$ or $\hat{5}$–$\hat{1}$–$\hat{5}$), it is just as common for these expositions to have two successive entries on the same pitch ($\hat{1}$–$\hat{5}$–$\hat{5}$, $\hat{1}$–$\hat{1}$–$\hat{5}$, or $\hat{5}$–$\hat{1}$–$\hat{1}$). *Fuga XXIV* is unusual because all three entries of the subject are centered around the fifth scale degree. The remaining three-part fugues begin with lengthier expositions that have four or five statements of the subject before reaching a cadence (for example, *Fuga XIII* and *Fuga XVIII*).

An exposition with four entries of the subject leading to a cadence is the most common scheme for the four-part fugues. *Fuga XXVIII* and *Fuga XXXV* have three entries leading to a cadence, while *Fuga XXIX*, *Fuga XXXII*, and *Fuga XXXIV* have five entries leading to a cadence. In some cases, the entries may be closely spaced (*Fuga XXV*), while in other four-part fugues the expositions are elongated by the use of free material interspersed between the last two statements of the subject (*Fuga XXX*). As in the three-part fugues, the pitch schemes for these opening entries vary; one of the most common schemes is entries centering around the pitches $\hat{5}$–$\hat{1}$–$\hat{1}$–$\hat{5}$. This pattern of entries is found in *Fuga XXV*, *Fuga XXVI*, *Fuga XXX*, and *Fuga XXXIII*. Klemm's favorite order of entries in his four-part fugues is tenor-bass-soprano-alto, although several other schemes are also found. The variety achieved in the opening sections of Klemm's fugues illustrates the fact that there is no particular order of subject and answer entries for fugues written during the seventeenth century.[31]

Whether it is a two-, three-, or four-part fugue, Klemm's compositions demonstrate one very important feature of the baroque fugue, which is that the initial entries of the subject in the various polyphonic lines will generally not begin before the last note of the previous subject statement is reached. This allows the fugue subject to be perceived by the listener without the interference of overlapping (or stretto) entries of the subject, as is generally the case with sixteenth-century imitative counterpoint. Such a wider spacing of entries was recommended by Gioseffo Zarlino, Pietro Pontio, and other late-sixteenth- and early-seventeenth-century theorists.[32] One of the few exceptions to this rule is the *Fuga XXVIII*, where Klemm has the bass entering halfway through the initial subject statement in the tenor line, and the alto entering halfway through the bass line's statement of the same subject in measures 1–4.

In most fugues, Klemm uses what would be later termed "real" entries, with all the notes of the subject being duplicated at the interval of the fifth. Although theorists state that such exact answers are most appropriate for subjects that are predominantly stepwise, Klemm employs this procedure even with subjects having interval skips. Only five of Klemm's fugues use "tonal" entries, with the first and fifth scale degrees complementing one another (for example, *Fuga X* and *Fuga XIII*). In his use of real entries of the subject, Klemm is consistent with the practice of his German colleagues, who did not regularly use tonal answers until the last decades of the seventeenth century.[33]

Procedures after the Exposition

After their opening expositions, Klemm's fugues proceed in a variety of ways. One of the most common of these procedures is that episodes are short. In his two- and three-part fugues, Klemm normally has one or two statements of the subject followed by from one to four measures of free material. Some of these two- and three-part fugues have passages with three or more entries of the subject before any free material is found. *Fuga VI*, for example, has six entries of the subject in a row; six of the three-part fugues have between three to seven entries of the subject before free material is found (see *Fuga XIII*, mm. 28–43). A fugue with an episode that is more than several measures long is a rare occurrence; one exception is *Fuga V*, which has an unusually long episode of five and one-half measures (mm. 23–28). In general, the four-part fugues have even less free material than their predecessors, with the subject being present at least 75 percent of the time.

Once the opening expositions have been completed, Klemm often writes statements of the subject centering around pitches other than the first and fifth scale degrees of the mode. Often these *commixtio modi* statements are centered on the second and fourth scale degrees, although several fugues have subject entries on the third or sixth scale degrees. The most interesting example of *commixtio modi* is found in *Fuga V*, which has entries on the third scale degree in measures 14–16 and 40–42, paired entries on the second and fifth scale degrees in measures 33–37 and 49–52, and paired entries on the first and fourth scale degrees in measures 44–47.[34] Klemm often solidifies these movements outside of the mode by having paired entries of the subject that are spaced a fifth apart. In measures 24–31 and 44–51 of *Fuga XI*, for example, there are paired entries of the subject on F and B♭ (first and fourth scale degrees) and on A and D (third and sixth scale degrees).

In their studies of fugue, both Imogene Horsley and Alfred Mann point out that one aesthetic ideal of seventeenth-century fugal composition was that the end of the work should be the most complex and exciting part.[35] This is reflected in approximately half of Klemm's fugues, which conclude with multiple statements of the subject in order to give his compositions greater rhetorical emphasis. *Fuga XXIV*, for example, ends with ten stretto statements of the subject, followed by two measures of closing cadential material in measures 67–81.

Stylistic Characteristics of the Fugues

Chromaticism and Dissonance Treatment

Most of the time, Klemm remains clearly within the modal scale chosen for a particular fugue. Accidentals are normally used only for cadences, to flatten the note above *la* in the hexachord, or to produce a major triad on or immediately after a cadential note. The three fugues in untransposed dorian/hypodorian mode (*Fuga I*, *Fuga XIV*, and *Fuga XXV*) have their cadences to D and A prepared by a C♯ and G♯, respectively; comparable alterations are made for the cadences to the first and fifth scale degrees in the G dorian/hypodorian fugues (*Fuga II*, *Fuga XIII*, and *Fuga XXVI*). The fugues utilizing this pair of modes have a flattened sixth scale degree (B♭ in untransposed dorian, E♭ in G dorian), either because it falls above the top note of the hexachord or to resolve the tritone between the third and sixth scale degrees. The dorian and hypodorian fugues use an occasional F♯ and B♮ to produce a major third above a cadential pitch or to accomodate an ascent to a G or C, respectively.

Occasionally, however, Klemm does use chromaticism and free dissonance, indicating that his fugues should not be viewed entirely as *stile antico* works. Chromaticism is particularly evident in the phrygian mode; his *Fuga III* has a G♯ and C♯ in the fugue subject, contradicting the character of the phrygian mode. Another example is *Fuga XXVII*, which has accidentals on four different pitches (F♯, G♯, C♯, A♯) that distort the character of the phrygian mode. The four-part fugue in the aeolian mode (*Fuga XXXIII*) has a freely composed chromatic figure on C♯–D–C♮ or G♯–A–G♮ that Klemm uses to avoid potential cadences.

In general, Klemm's fugues are characterized by the careful dissonance treatment associated with the *stile antico*. A cursory examination of his *Fuga I*, for example, shows that dissonances are prepared and left as passing or neighbor tones, or as suspensions resolving to a cadential leading-tone.

There are some occasions when Klemm uses the type of free dissonance treatment found in the *stile moderno*. Suspensions are normally used as isolated dissonances that prepare a cadence, but there are times when three or more suspensions in a row are found (for example, *Fuga VII*, mm. 36–38). Dissonant anticipations and skips either to or from a dissonance, another *stile moderno* trait, are used in a large number of fugues (for example, *Fuga X*, mm. 60–61, and *Fuga VIII*, mm. 28–29). Although not very commonplace, two dissonances in a row are found in several fugues (for example, *Fuga XXXIII*, mm. 75–77); diminutions are rare (for example, *Fuga XXXII*, mm. 4–18).

Melodic and Rhythmic Variation

One of the most interesting aspects of Klemm's fugues is the numerous melodic and rhythmic alterations that he makes. Melodic alterations are normally made during the middle or latter portions of the subject, so that the identity of the subject's opening is preserved. In several fugues, the last note of the subject is altered from a descending fourth or fifth to an ascending second, or from a descending second to a descending fifth or an ascending second (for example, *Fuga XXIV*, mm. 45–47). In *Fuga I*, the penultimate note of the subject is altered in measures 16–17 and in measures 39–41 to form a perfect (major sixth to octave) cadence. Sometimes a note group in the latter portion of the subject is also changed. In *Fuga XIII*, the last three or four notes of the subject are changed on two occasions (mm. 34–36, 47–50); in *Fuga XXXIII*, the last five notes of the subject are altered frequently (mm. 18–26, 35–37, 45–61, 87–90).

Melodic alterations during the beginning or middle portions of the fugue subject are rarely found. One example is the last three-part fugue (*Fuga XXIV*), where Klemm changes the third and fourth notes of the subject from a descending fourth to an ascending second (mm. 53–55, 58–64).[36] In one four-part fugue, he alters the third through fifth notes of the subject from a descending fifth and an ascending octave to a descending fourth/fifth followed by an ascending fourth/fifth (*Fuga XXXIII*, mm. 23, 47, 75, 80, 88). Two fugues have melodic alterations accommodating stretto duet entries (*Fuga VI*, mm. 32–38; *Fuga XXX*, mm. 59–65).

One special type of melodic alteration, inversion of the subject, is used on numerous occasions—the only change that effects the entire fugue subject. For examples of inversion, see *Fuga XI* (mm. 9–16, 22–30, 35–37, 40–47, 54–64) and *Fuga XVI* (mm. 20–33, 39–44, 53–63, 75–77, 82–84). In general, Klemm uses inversion of the subject more frequently than his contemporaries. An examination of ten ricercars by Frescobaldi shows that inversion of the opening subject is used in only one composition, while none of Steigleder's ricercars utilize this technique.[37]

Rhythmic alterations may include the lengthening or shortening of individual notes, augmentation or diminution of several notes of the subject, or syncopation. As in the case of melodic alterations, these rhythmic changes are usually applied to part of the subject rather than to the entire subject. Klemm sometimes diminishes the value of the first several notes of the subject or augments the latter portion of the subject, and may use both techniques during the same passage (for example, *Fuga III*, mm. 36–47). In several fugues augmentation at the conclusion of the piece gives the fugue a greater sense of finality (for example, *Fuga XXX*, mm. 72–76). As the ricercars of Frescobaldi and Steigleder indicate, such partial or complete rhythmic alterations of a subject were fairly common in the early seventeenth century.[38]

Klemm's penchant for stretto entries of the subject also leads to many examples of augmentation, diminution, or syncopation. Rhythmic alterations made for this purpose can be found in *Fuga VIII* (mm. 63–71) and *Fuga XXVII* (mm. 39–44, 50–53). *Fuga XVIII* is an excellent example of the simultaneous use of syncopation, diminution of the opening three notes, and augmentation during multiple entries of the subject (mm. 16–19, 24–47).

Cadential Pitches

The choice of cadential pitches in Klemm's fugues provides evidence for the trend from modality to emerging tonality. In the dorian, lydian, and ionian pairs of modes (modes 1–2, 5–6, 11–12), the cadences are equally distributed between the first and fifth scale degrees, helping to establish a polarity between tonic and dominant. Occasionally there are cadences on the third or fourth scale degrees; cadences on the second, sixth, or seventh degrees are nonexistent in the dorian modes, and rare in the lydian and ionian modes.

The fugues written in the other modes most frequently have cadences to the final of the mode. In the mixolydian pair of modes (modes 7–8), there are only half as many cadences on the fifth scale degree as there are on the final of the mode, and the unstable third scale degree is generally avoided in favor of cadences on the fourth scale degree; these are the only three scale degrees used. In the aeolian pair of modes (modes 9–10), cadences on the fourth scale degree are at least as common as those on the third and fifth degrees. The problematic phrygian pair of modes (modes 3–4) has a wide variety of cadential pitches, with cadences on the fourth, sixth, or seventh scale degrees being found as well as ones on the third or fifth degrees. With cadences on the fourth scale degree almost as common as those on the final of the mode, only the second scale degree is avoided in the phrygian modes. Klemm's cadences on the various scale degrees are summarized in table 1.

The data shown in the column totals for table 1 illustrates that Klemm's fugues exhibit what some theorists have called a "solar" relationship, that is, one in which the first scale degree tends to be a strong focal point of attention. But with the exception of the phrygian, hypophrygian, and aeolian modes, the data also indicate an emerging interest in the dominant. Particularly in the case of the dorian, lydian, and ionian pairs of modes, there is a strong tendency to establish a polarity between dominant and tonic that helps to define the tonal center of the mode.

Klemm's Idea of the Fugue

During Klemm's lifetime, the thematically unified Renaissance fantasia and ricercar was gradually evolving into the seventeenth-century fugue. His *Partitura* could thus be seen as an attempt to clarify the concept of what a fugue should be at a time when ideas were not yet standardized. Viewed in this light, one could use Klemm's fugues to devise the following set of rules for writing early-seventeenth-century fugues:

1. The subject should be easily perceived as a full-length entity.

2. This subject must be presented consistently during the course of a fugue, with only short episodes to separate statements.

3. The first and fifth scale degrees of the mode should be emphasized, both in the subjects and in the ensuing cadences.

4. A fugue should be conservative in its use of chromaticism and treatment of dissonance.

5. The exposition may have one or two entries of the subject for each participating polyphonic line.

TABLE 1
Cadential Pitches in the Various Modes

Mode	Scale Degree						
	1	2	3	4	5	6	7
1 (dorian)	18	0	3	0	22	0	0
2 (hypodorian)	18	0	3	2	18	0	0
3 (phrygian)	13	0	4	11	3	2	0
4 (hypophrygian)	16	0	5	12	6	5	2
5 (lydian)	23	1	3	4	22	1	1
6 (hypolydian)	16	0	3	2	10	2	0
7 (mixolydian)	30	0	0	5	11	0	0
8 (hypomixolydian)	22	0	0	4	8	0	0
9 (aeolian)	27	0	2	12	2	1	0
10 (hypoaeolian)	17	0	3	1	6	0	1
11 (ionian)	19	0	2	1	13	1	0
12 (hypoionian)	19	1	0	0	22	0	0
Totals	238	2	28	54	143	12	4

6. These subject statements in the exposition may take place on any combination of first and fifth scale degree entries.

7. During the middle portion of the fugue, the subject may occasionally enter on other pitches besides the first and fifth scale degrees.

8. After the exposition, a good fugue should modify the character of the subject by altering some melodic intervals, changing the rhythms of small note groups, inverting the subject, using augmentation or diminution, and employing stretto entries to add intensity at certain moments.

In Klemm's works, the fugue is already viewed as a complex rhetorical statement, one that begins by clearly stating the topic for discourse, and continues by reiterating the topic as it is cleverly expounded upon and developed.

Notes on Performance

One of the most intriguing aspects of Klemm's fugues is the flexibility of performance medium, the fact that most of these compositions sound effectively on so many other instruments in addition to the organ. Some of the most likely ensembles for Klemm's fugues would be consorts of recorders, transverse flutes, dulcians, cornetts and sackbutts, viols, or members of the violin family. All of these instruments are represented in the first volume of Schütz's *Symphoniae Sacrae*, which was published two years before Klemm's *Partitura*. Eight of the two-part fugues work well on tenor and bass recorders (*Fuga II, IV, V, VI, VII, IX, XI,* and *XII*); all of the two-part fugues could be played on tenor and bass viols, although the second and tenth fugues would lie best on treble and tenor viols (this would avoid playing on or above the top fret). The three-part fugues fall within the ranges of the soprano, tenor, and bass recorders, viols, cornetts or sackbutts, and several other instruments; many of their top parts would lie more comfortably on the violin than on the treble viol (particularly *Fuga XIII, XIV, XV, XVI, XIX, XXIII,* and *XXIV*). The bass parts of the four-part fugues lie between F and e', a comfortable range for the bass members of the viol, dulcian, or sackbutt families; the remaining polyphonic lines fit on the tenor, alto, and soprano members of these instrument families.

Cadential ornamentation would probably be a stylistically appropriate addition to Klemm's fugues. In some fugues, Klemm writes sixteenth-note figurations that stop two or three beats before a cadence, in whatever line that carries the ascending half-step to the cadential note. It seems unlikely that Klemm would want the rhythmic momentum of a phrase to stop so abruptly, and more likely that he did not write figurations for these cadential approaches because improvised ornamentation was assumed during such situations (for example, *Fuga XII,* mm. 21–24). For examples of stylistically appropriate cadential ornaments, one of the best sources is the keyboard ricercars, fantasias, and fugues of Klemm's teacher, Christian Erbach.[39]

Appendix

Preface

Floruit hac tenus in nostra Germania, plures per annos, Tabulatura illa Organica, constans suis literis & characteribus. Floruit bono suo & non contemnendo. Tabulatura alia Italis in usu fuit. Vocant Partituram, & conflata est ex propriis & usitatis sonorum signis. Elapso tempore in Patriam nostram allata est. Visa à peritioribus Musicis, & approbata fuit. Etenim inventa firmioris fundaminis, melioris utilitatis, majoris necessitatis. Et ut unicum saltem tangam. Bassus Generalis seu Continuus iam nunc in omnibus præstantioribus Choris Musicis usurpatur. Offertur etiam Organœdis. Quam anxiè sudant in illo, qui ejusmodi signorum plane ignati. In hac Tabulatura ego privati mei studii ergò, composui quasdam Fuga's 2. 3. & 4. Vocibus, ad duodecim consuetos Tonos Musicos. Auditæ sunt á nonnullis: suaserunt illi, ut publici juris facerem. Genueram quidem eas non in hanc spem: cùm tamen hicata volebant, feci tandem & emisi. Sed hac lege, ut omnes sciant, me dilcentibus, non doctis, Tironibus, non Magistris, hac composuisse. Dedicavi autem istas V. Illustr. Celsit, Excelso Nomini. Vocavit me huc Amor ille coelittis missus, erga divinam Musicam, ex quo, V. Illustr: Celsit: Nobiliss: Præfecto, Volrado á Wazdorff suasore, celeberrimo verò Schuzio, Magni Parentis Archi. Phonasco, Informatore, ipsa sanctum Musices studium, per dictam Tabulaturam Italicam exercet. Vocavit me huc magnum Beneficium, quo V. Illustr: Celsit: me, ipsi Madrigalia nuper emissa, offerentem, Clementer affecit. V. Illust: Celsit: ergò rogo humilima subjectione, ut hoc le vidense & exiguum animi & cultus devoti munus, clementer accipiat. Mihi enim, quem coetera destituunt, nihil praeter munera haec mentis servitia & vota. Deus Jehova V. Illust. Celsit: faciat Patriæ longævam ac valentem! Dabatur Dresdæ, die 6 Februarij, quo haberi coepit Lipsiat celebratissimus ille Procerum Evangelicorum Conventus, qui universæ, Ecclesiæ Reiq; publicæ Christianæ auspicatus & salutaris esse velit/ Anno 1631.

V. Illust. Celsitud.
Subjectiss:
JOHANNES KLEMMIUS.

Instrumental tablature, its letters and characters fixed, flourished for many years here in our Germany. It was valued for its own goodness and should not be looked down upon. Another type of tablature was found in Italy. There they call it Partituram, and it was molded from appropriate and familiar notated sounds. It was brought to our country in the time of our fathers. It has been examined by skilled musicians, and has been approved of. And indeed, this invention strengthened the very foundations [of music] and was considered more appropriate, a greater necessity. In any event, it has remained as the only attainable solution of the time. Already the general-bass or continuo is being used in all outstanding music choirs. It is also being encountered by instrumentalists. Much as all were disturbed and made anxious by this discovery, since figures of that kind were simply unknown, I therefore spent some of my private time in this manner studying the tablature, composing 2, 3, and 4-voiced fugues in the twelve customary musical modes. Some of them have been heard, so that well-known advisers have valued them at public juries. And so they have been thought to have been finally made, with yet this wish that they be sent out from here. Yet this present collection, as all know, has been selected by me, not the learned Tironibus, and not arranged by our director. Indeed I am dedicating the work to the most illustrious and noblest, who is called the most highest. Cupid, the god of love, called me to be in company with those sent from heaven, towards the heavenly musicians. The work is dedicated to: the highest, noblest, the commander, Volrado the counselor from Wazdorff, and truly also to the distinguished Schütz, the great parents of music. The singing teacher gave shape to his studies of sacred music by employing the aforementioned Italian tablature. This great or noble service where I have been called, noblest and merciful ruler, I dedicate to you these madrigals that have not long ago been set forth. To our illustrious ruler: I therefore ask that what is humbly placed below, as it is seen, is given life to a small extent and cultivated by devoted citizens, so that it is gradually accepted. To me, however, nothing was more of a new gift than the abandonment of the devotion to the slavery of the soul. To God Jehova and our most illustrious leader: May our country live a long time and grow strong! This work is given to Dresden, on the sixth day of February, when Lipsius began to host these great gatherings for the long sessions of evangelization, which are universal in nature, for Reiq churches, and for all Christians who are consecrated and wish to be saved. In the year 1631.

To our illustrious ruler,
your subject,
Johann Klemm.

Postscript

Ad Lectorem Philomusum

In quem finem, Lector Philomuse, hoc opusculum emiserim, ex Dedicatione videre potes. In ipsis Fugis, chromatibus & diminutionibus abstinui, ne opusculum nimium excresceret. Si aliis Instrumentis eas canere lubet, singulæ voces seorsim scribendæ erunt. Tantum est, quod to monere volui. Vale & meum laborem boni consule.

Autor.

To the reader of the muses.

In that which is bound here, reader, this work that has been sent forth, you have been able to see since the dedication. In these fugues, chromaticism and diminutions are avoided, and are not used excessively. And if you wish to play them on all instruments, they have been written out in single voices. It is so because you may wish to instruct yourself. Goodbye and may my efforts be thought well of.

The author.

Notes

1. *The New Grove Dictionary of Music and Musicians,* s.v. "Klemm, Johann," by Alexander Silbiger.

2. See Christian Erbach, *Collected Keyboard Compositions,* ed. Clare G. Rayner (Rome: American Institute of Musicology, 1971), 1:ix.

3. Joshua Rifkin and Colin Timms, "Heinrich Schütz," in *The New Grove North European Baroque Masters* (New York: Norton, 1985), 8.

4. Gina Spagnoli, "Dresden at the Time of Heinrich Schütz," in *The Early Baroque Era: From the Late 16th Century to the 1660s,* ed. Curtis Price (Englewood Cliffs, N.J.: Prentice Hall, 1994), 164–65.

5. Hans Joachim Moser, *Heinrich Schütz: His Life and Work,* trans. Carl Pfatteicher (St. Louis: Concordia, 1959), 94.

6. Spagnoli, "Dresden of Heinrich Schütz," 168–69.

7. Ibid., 165–68.

8. Moser, *Schütz,* 183–84.

9. Ibid., 182.

10. His first partnership was with the Leipzig organist Daniel Weixer; later he collaborated with Alexander Hering in Bautzen.

11. Silbiger, "Klemm." See also *Die Musik und Geschichte in Gegenwart,* s.v. "Klemm, Johann," by Friedrich Wilhelm Riedel.

12. Gina Spagnoli, *Letters and Documents of Heinrich Schütz, 1656–1672: An Annotated Translation* (Ann Arbor: UMI Research Press, 1990), 7, 14.

13. Ibid., 92.

14. See *The New Grove Dictionary of Music and Musicians,* s.v. "Fugue," by Roger Bullivant.

15. Willi Apel, *The History of Keyboard Music to 1700* (Bloomington: Indiana University Press, 1972), devotes two brief paragraphs on p. 386 to a discussion of the tonal structure of the fugal expositions of Klemm's fugues.

16. Beginning with the 1573 edition of his treatise, Zarlino placed the ionian mode first.

17. Samuel Scheidt, *Tabulatura nova* (Hamburg, 1624); Johann Ulrich Steigleder, *Tabulaturbuch* (Strasbourg, 1627). Other major printed collections continued to use tablature; these include Johann Woltz's *Nova musices organicae tabulatura* (Basel, 1617) and Johannes Erasmus Kindermann's *Harmonia organica* (Nuremberg, 1645).

18. "si aliis Instrumentus eas canere lubet, singulae voces seursim scribendae erunt."

19. "in ipsis Fugis, chromatibus & diminutionibus abstinui, ne opusculum nimium excresceret."

20. "Auditae sunt a nonnullis: suaserunt illi, ut publici juris facerem."

21. Thomas Stoltzer, *Ausgewählte Werke,* ed. Hans Albrecht, Das Erbe Deutscher Musik, 22 (Frankfurt: Peters, 1942).

22. Costanzo Antegnati, *L'Antegnata intavolature de ricercari d'organo,* ed. Willi Apel (Rome: American Institute of Musicology, 1965); Erbach, *Keyboard Compositions.*

23. Costanzo Festa, *Counterpoints on a Cantus Firmus,* ed. Richard Agee, Recent Researches in the Music of the Renaissance, 107 (Madison: A-R Editions, 1997), x.

24. This is also the case with many of Frescobaldi's ricercars; see Girolamo Frescobaldi, *Orgel- und Klavierwerke,* ed. Pierre Pidoux (Kassel: Bärenreiter, 1971), 2:56–80.

25. Benito Rivera, *German Music Theory in the Early Seventeenth Century: The Treatises of Johannes Lippius* (Ann Arbor: UMI Press, 1980), 199–205.

26. Imogene Horsley, *Fugue: History and Practice* (New York: Free Press, 1966), 75–78.

27. Frescobaldi, *Orgel- und Klavierwerke,* 2:62.

28. See Simon Lohet, *Compositions for Organ,* ed. Larry Peterson (Rome: American Institute of Musicology, 1976), 37–38. This fugue was published in Johann Woltz's *Novae musices organicae tabulatura* of 1617, one of the best-known organ publications of the time.

29. Alfred Mann, *The Study of Fugue* (New Brunswick, N.J.: Rutgers University Press, 1958), 42.

30. Joel Lester, *Between Modes and Keys: German Theory 1592–1802* (Stuyvesant, N.Y.: Pendragon Press, 1989), 13–15.

31. Horsley, *Fugue,* 159.

32. Horsley, *Fugue,* 162–63 and Gioseffo Zarlino, *The Art of Counterpoint: Part Three of Le istitutioni harmoniche (1558),* trans. Guy Marco and Claude Palisca (New Haven: Yale University Press, 1968), 127–29. For a more conservative approach to fugal imitation, see Lohet, *Compositions for Organ,* 23–29, where the opening entries of the subject generally overlap with one another.

33. Horsley, *Fugue,* 79.

34. Other examples of this significant style trait are as follows: *Fuga IV,* two entries on the third scale degree, mm. 31–35; *Fuga VI,* one partial entry on the fourth scale degree, mm. 48–49; *Fuga IX,* one partial entry on the fourth scale degree, mm. 49–50; *Fuga XIII,* one entry on the fourth scale degree and two entries on the second scale degree, mm. 41–50; *Fuga XVI,* two inverted entries on the fourth scale degree, mm. 25–28; *Fuga XVIII,* paired entries on the second and fifth scale degrees, mm. 24–28 and 42–45; *Fuga XXIII,* paired entries on the second and fifth scale degrees, mm. 31–34; *Fuga XXVII,* paired entries on the first and fourth scale degrees, mm. 49–55; *Fuga XXVIII,* four entries on the fourth scale degree, mm. 26–35; *Fuga XXIX,* one entry on the fourth scale degree, mm. 63–65; *Fuga XXX,* paired entries on the second and fifth scale degrees, mm. 57–61 and 71–74; *Fuga XXXI,* one entry on the fourth scale degree, mm. 45–48.

35. Horsley, *Fugue,* 228; Mann, *Study of Fugue,* 43–45.

36. This particular alteration appears to be a choice on Klemm's part, rather than a requirement of the counterpoint. While there are stretto duet entries at this point in the fugue, the counterpoint between the two parts carrying statements of the subject would still work out if Klemm had not changed the third and fourth notes of the subject.

37. Frescobaldi, *Orgel- und Klavierwerke*, 2:59; Johann Ulrich Steigleder, *Compositions for Keyboard*, ed. Willi Apel (Rome: American Institute of Musicology, 1969), 2:1–75.

38. Frescobaldi, *Orgel- und Klavierwerke*, 2:56, 62, 65, 74, and 80; Steigleder, *Compositions for Keyboard*, 2:1, 11, 21, 29, 36, 55, and 62.

39. For an example, see the "Fuga primi toni" in Erbach, *Keyboard Compositions*, 3:13–16 (cadential ornaments appear in mm. 8, 12, 16, 20, 24, 28, 33, 36, 39, 43, 48, 52, 56, 62, 66, 77, and 79 in this fugue).

Plate 1. *Partitura seu Tabulatura italica*, 1631, title page. Reprinted with permission of the Herzog August Bibliothek, Wolfenbüttel.

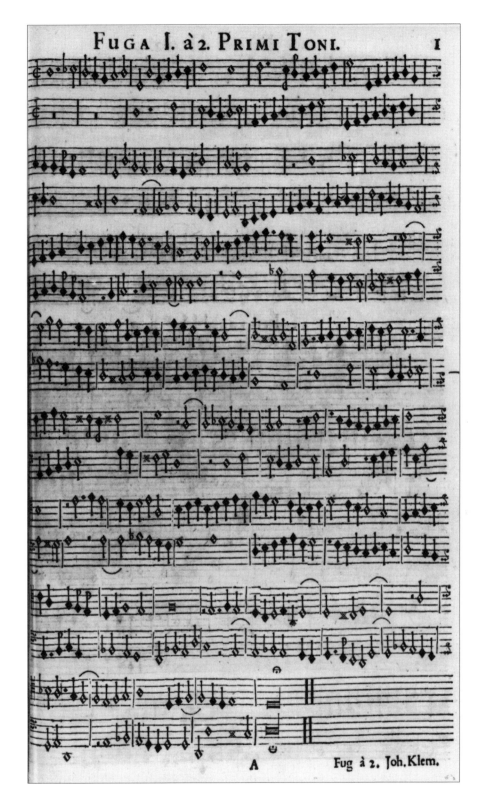

Plate 2. *Partitura seu Tabulatura italica, Fuga I primi toni*, p. 1. Reprinted with permission of the Herzog August Bibliothek, Wolfenbüttel.

Fuga I. à 2. Primi Toni

Fuga II. à 2. Secundi Toni

3

Fuga III. à 2. Tertii Toni

Fuga IV. à 2. Quarti Toni

8

Fuga V. à 2. Quinti Toni

Fuga VI. à 2. Sexti Toni

Fuga VII. à 2. Septimi Toni

Fuga VIII. à 2. Octavi Toni

Fuga IX. à 2. Noni Toni

Fuga X. à 2. Decimi Toni

22

Fuga XI. à 2. Undecimi Toni

23

Fuga XII. à 2. Duodecimi Toni

Fuga XIII. à 3. Primi Toni

Fuga XIV. à 3. Secundi Toni

Fuga XV. à 3. Tertii Toni

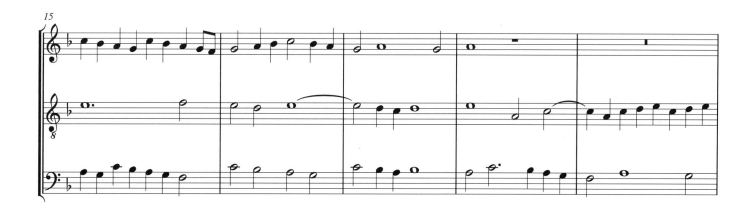

Fuga XVI. à 3. Quarti Toni

Fuga XVII. à 3. Quinti Toni

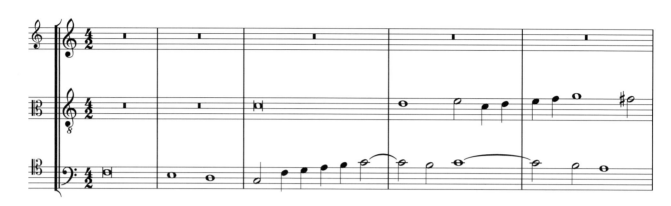

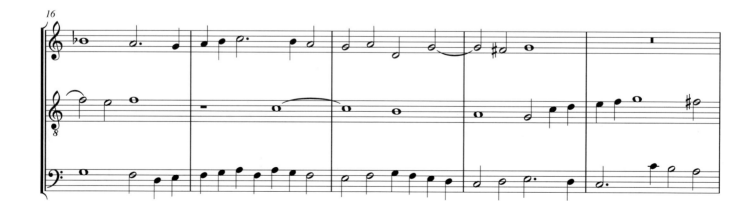

Fuga XVIII. à 3. Sexti Toni

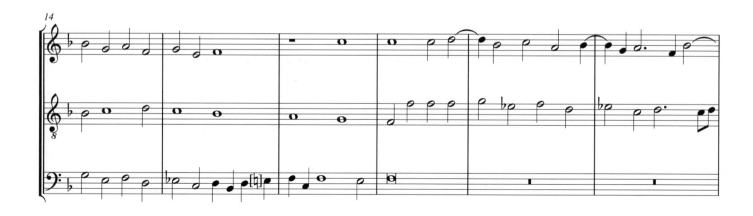

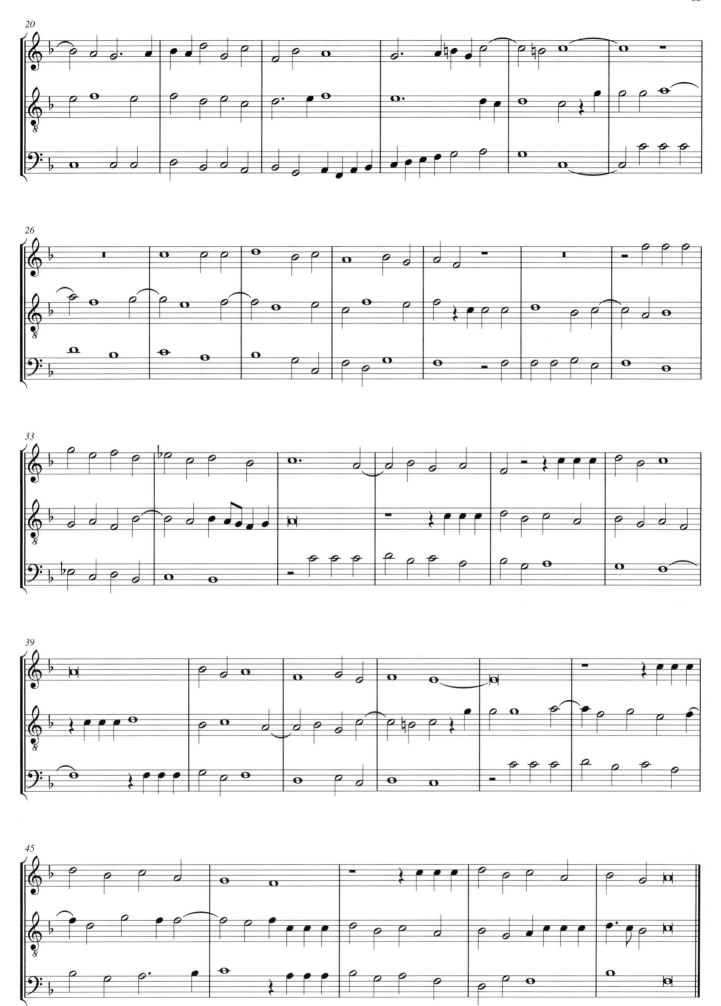

44

Fuga XIX. à 3. Septimi Toni

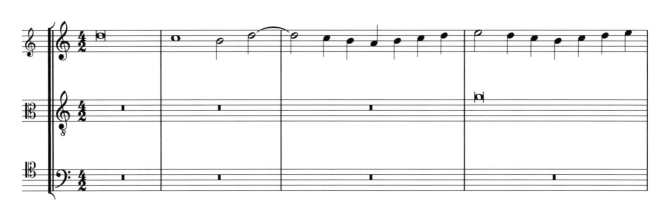

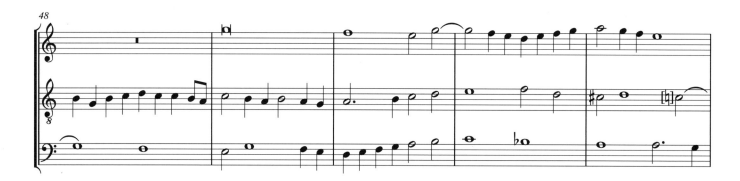

Fuga XX. à 3. Octavi Toni

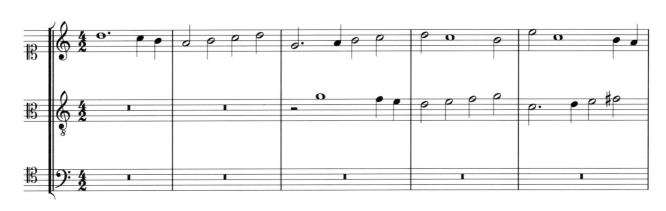

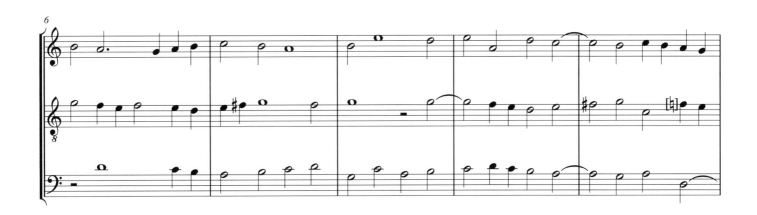

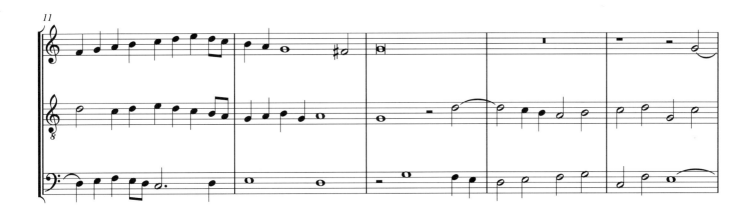

Fuga XXI. à 3. Noni Toni

Fuga XXII. à 3. Decimi Toni

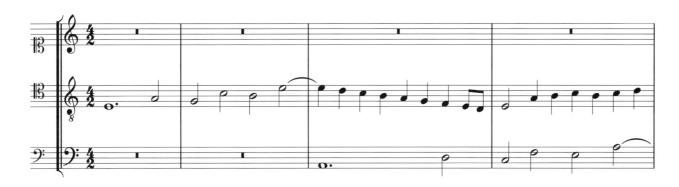

54

Fuga XXIII. à 3. Undecimi Toni

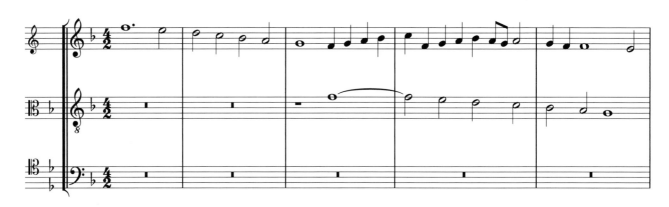

Fuga XXIV. à 3. Duodecimi Toni

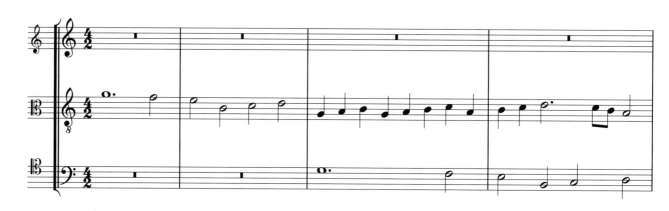

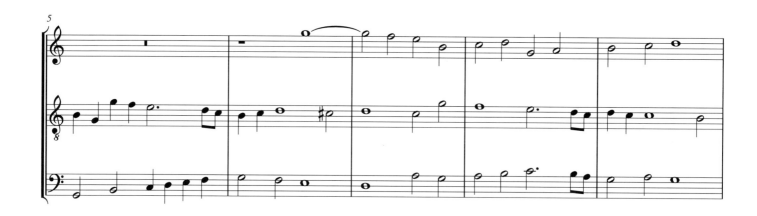

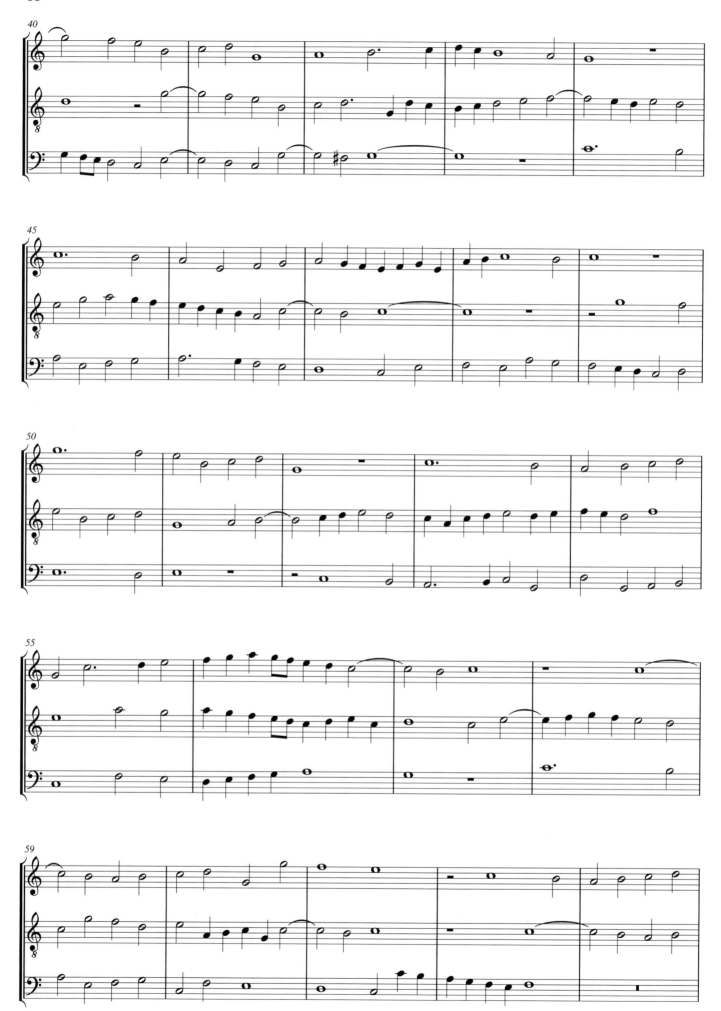

Fuga XXV. à 4. Primi Toni

Fuga XXVI. à 4. Secundi Toni

Fuga XXVII. à 4. Tertii Toni

Fuga XXVIII. à 4. Quarti Toni

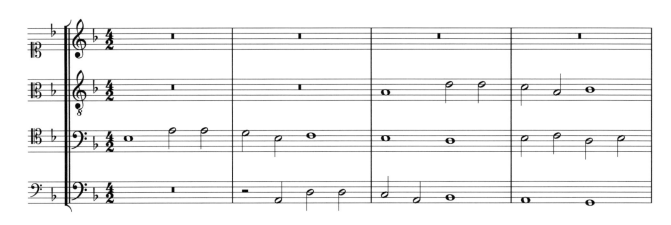

72

73

Fuga XXIX. à 4. Quinti Toni

Fuga XXX. à 4. Sexti Toni

Fuga XXXI. à 4. Septimi Toni

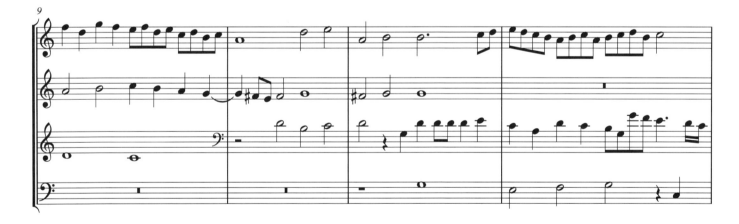

Fuga XXXII. à 4. Octavi Toni

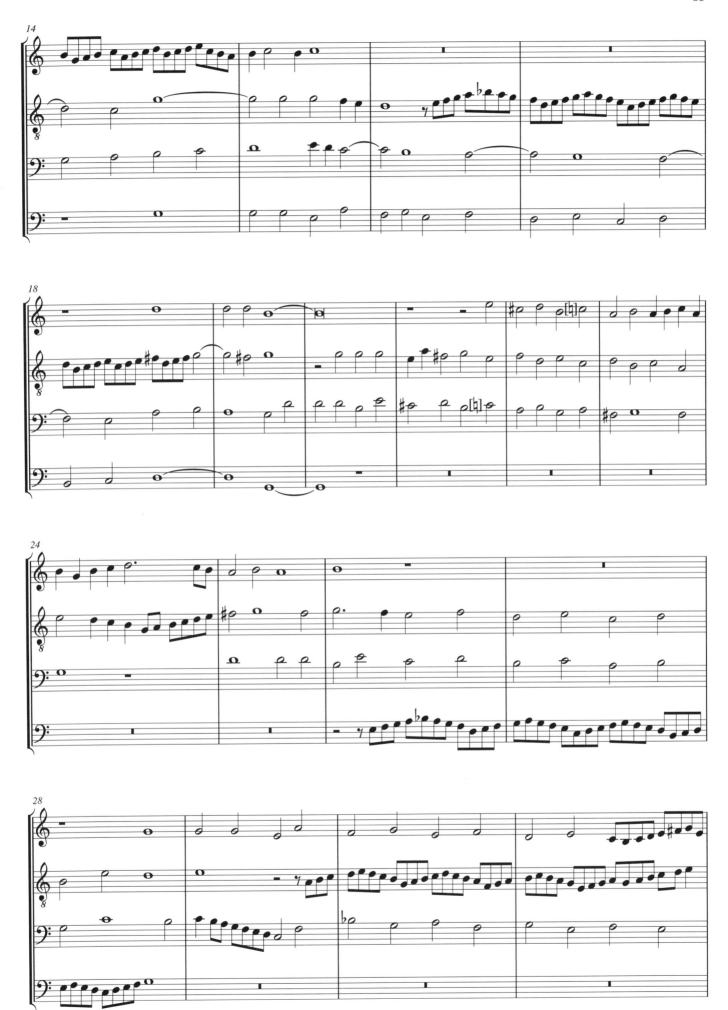

Fuga XXXIII. à 4. Noni Toni

92

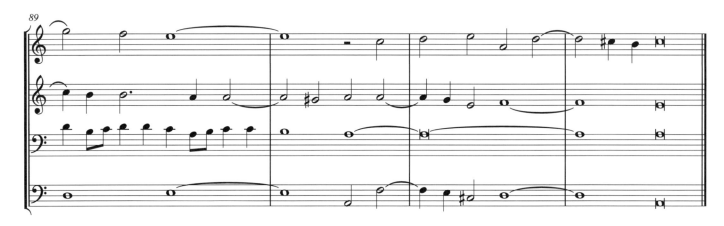

Fuga XXXIV. à 4. Decimi Toni

Fuga XXXV. à 4. Undecimi Toni

Fuga XXXVI. à 4. Duodecimi Toni

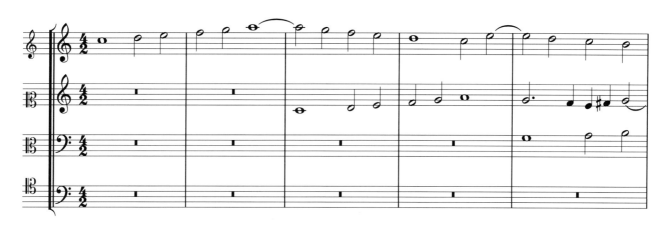

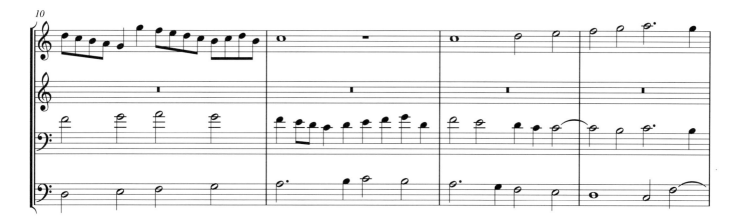

Critical Report

Source

This edition is based on a copy of the 1631 *Partitura seu Tabulatura italica* that can be found in the Zwickau Ratsschulbibliothek (RISM K 894); the microfilm copy used by this editor was obtained from the Deutsches Musikgeschichtliches Archiv in Kassel. There are no other printed or manuscript sources for Klemm's fugues. The only two extant copies of the print are found in Zwickau and in the Herzog August Bibliothek, Wolfenbüttel.

As indicated by the title, the *Partitura* is in open score format, with each page numbered separately using arabic numerals. On facing pages such as pages 2–3, the music is printed from left to right across both pages before moving to the next staff system. The Latin preface has been given in the introduction with a translation. After the conclusion of the last fugue there is a brief but important postscript on page 90 (also translated), which is signed "Autor." This is followed by a list of errata on the bottom of the page, and on page 91, the inscription "Soli Deo Gloria: Finis."

Editorial Methods

In his *Partitura*, Klemm indicates each fugue by its mode, its numerical position in the print (in roman numerals), and its number of polyphonic parts. In this edition, the original titles have been retained and tacitly regularized.

The open score format of the original has been retained, facilitating ensemble performance, as well as study of the fugues for pedagogical purposes. Keyboard arrangements of the fugues have been published separately as a supplement to this volume. Clefs and key signatures of the source are provided by incipits. The readings of the errata have been tacitly accepted.

Barlines have been given as in the original print, except that on the right-hand side of each page barlines are usually not printed but marked off by a sign indicating the end of the staff system. In such cases, barlines have been added. In half of the fugues, there are occasional measures with either two or six beats rather than four; the pulse should remain constant here, since these places occur only at the end of a staff system on the recto pages of the source or before the final note of the composition. The note values of the original edition have been retained, and the consistently used time indication of a semicircle with a line through it has been replaced with the signature $\frac{4}{2}$.

Five changes have been made to the rhythmic notation of the original print:

1. In the 1631 source, each final note is a *longa* with a fermata; these pitches have been notated here as breves without a fermata, and it should be understood that the length of the final note can vary somewhat at the performer's discretion.

2. When the last note of a measure is held over into the next measure for half of its original note value, this is normally indicated by a dotted note in the source. In this edition a dotted whole note extending across the barline has been indicated as a whole note tied to a half note, and a dotted half note extending across the barline has been written as a half note tied to a quarter note. One example of this can be found in the alto line of *Fuga XXVI*, measures 62–64.

3. When a break between the left- and right-hand sides of the page occurs during the middle of a measure, the notes and rests extending over to the other side of the page are usually divided. Here they are notated as they would be if there were no page break. One example is *Fuga XXI*, where in measure 31 the treble and bass lines have dotted half notes that are notated in the source as a half note tied to a quarter note due to a page break. Another example is *Fuga XXVI*, where in measure 34 the breve rest in the treble line and the whole note in the tenor line are indicated by two whole rests and two tied-over half notes, respectively, due to the page break.

4. There are several instances where dotted quarter notes are followed by three eighth notes. In such cases, the dotted quarter note has been indicated as a quarter note tied to an eighth note that becomes the beginning of a group of four eighth notes. For an example, see the treble line of *Fuga XXXIV*, measure 41.

5. In the original print, eighth notes appear as separately flagged notes. Here they have been beamed together according to modern practice.

The usage of accidentals has also been altered to conform to modern practice. In the original, accidentals are good only for the note that they are assigned to; here they are valid for the entire measure, and they are cancelled at the completion of the measure. When a pitch previously altered occurs later within the same measure with no alteration, the appropriate sign of cancellation is added in brackets, since there is no such indication in the 1631 print. In the bass line of *Fuga VII*, for example, both of the F's in measure 12 are marked with a sharp sign in the source, whereas in measure 14 only the first F is marked with a sharp sign, meaning that the second F is understood to be natural. The editorial practice followed here is to place a sharp sign in measure 12 only on the first F in the measure, and to cancel the sharp sign in the latter part of measure 14 with a bracketed natural sign.

Critical Notes

In the notes, generic voice names have been used to designate the parts—soprano, alto, tenor, and bass—depending on the range. Pitches are identified using the system in which middle C = c′.

Fuga IX

M. 31, barline missing (or too faint to read) in source.

Fuga XI

Mm. 59–60, soprano, tie over quarter and half note c″s in m. 59 of source; it has been moved so that it occurs from the last half note in m. 59 to the first half note of m. 60.

Fuga XVII

M. 60, soprano, note 1 is d′.

Fuga XXV

Mm. 67–68, soprano, there is a fermata over the penultimate note as well as over the last note of the fugue.

Fuga XXXI

M. 15, beat 3, bass, and m. 26, beat 4, tenor, quarter note b's have natural signs.

RECENT RESEARCHES IN THE MUSIC OF THE BAROQUE ERA
Christoph Wolff, general editor